THE INTROVERTED ARTIST'S GUIDE

TO

ART SALES

BY

DONTAE T. MUSE

Preface

Let me get this out of the way. I do not have a background consisting of any type of formal art training. All that I have is the knowledge that I have obtained and what I will share in this book was learned through self-education, mentors, and most importantly, mistakes. I actually have never even taken a basic art class and could actually benefit from one considering my lackluster skills in shading. I do have a Master's degree, but it is in Public Administration not in Fine Arts, Art Education, or Art History.

I do have practical business experience however. I have previously started a couple of other businesses before opening my own art gallery. The first was an event planning company in which I now use my experience, relationships, and acquired skills to host events in my gallery. The second was a direct marketing and sales company in which I managed nineteen independent sales contractors. I taught them all many sales techniques and operated the business for almost three years before getting burned out by the seventy plus hour work weeks. Even a couple of hours of my Sunday (the only day we closed) were spent on getting prepared for the upcoming week. The last is my fast growing visual artist professional development company, *I Am D. Muse.*

Outside of these ventures I have had stints being an employee with multiple employers. I have never stayed with one employer for more than a couple of years. Part of that was that once the learning curve was done and I learned about all I could in my position I would become bored or disinterested in my position. If there was no way to move up expeditiously without someone else having to get promoted, fired, or die in order for the position to open, that was typically the signal for me to part ways. I would soon either quit or get fired.

I have done a range of things as an employee from retirement investments for Metropolitan Life to credit and loans as a personal banker with Wells Fargo to car sales with a large dealer to teaching at an institution of higher learning and so on. Going through all of this I do not know if I was trying to "find myself" or not. In hindsight, I now realize that every experience along my path has prepared me for today even more than my traditional education. If I didn't have a sharp edge to me I would consider myself a well-rounded individual. When it came to the sales aspect in any position I naturally thrived and improved with the more I learned through study and experience.

So, how did I end up in the art world you ask? That's a good question. Thanks for asking. I have to keep telling the story over and over to myself because it is still hard to believe that I pulled it off, especially at the level of success we are heading to. The short answer is that I just fell into it.

As a child I could barely draw a stick figure. If I had a ruler to help keep the line straight then I would fare a little better but drawing "Hangman" was the furthest my visual art skills and talent would take me back then. I would even visit my local public library to get books on how to draw this and how to draw that only to have my renderings look absolutely nothing like what I attempted to draw even though I had a step-by-step manual with very clear instructions. My circles were oval. My squares were rectangular. It just wasn't working out for me and it definitely deterred my seriously having any involvement with visual art. I finally gave up on art and being an artist around fourteen years old.

My journey in visual art began when my partner in my music production and artist development company and I were preparing to shoot a music video. The video was for a song done by one of our artists and featured another relatively known artist in hip-hop at the time. Knowing that a visual for the song would help push the song and that it could possibly be seen by many people I was personally determined to make my mark not only with the song but also with my individual style of fashion.

The only way to be the only one who owns something is that there has to be only one in existence. With that understanding I recruited a lifetime artist friend of ours to create a custom design on a pair of sneakers for me so I could stand out in the music video. I gave him the sneakers and he produced a one-of-a-kind splatter paint pattern on them with the same colors of some special socks that I would also be wearing in the video to complete my outfit.

My partner in music and I were already getting ready to begin our search for a larger space to house our business. We needed a space where we could host events and also move our small recording studio setup to. We had grown tired of being at the mercy of the owners of the establishments that we used for our events. We needed to be able to have control of our own space.

Upon mentioning this plan to our artist friend he mentioned that he was also looking for a space to start a business. He was looking to open up his own art gallery. I came up with the bright idea that we should all team up and open an art gallery together large enough to host events. It was then that the seed was planted.

Now, here is our first HUGE hiccup in that plan. Once I had scouted many options and finally found our future location, received an "ok" on it from our artist friend, negotiated the lease terms, filed incorporation paperwork for the business, and started spreading the word about our new endeavor my artist friend then decides that this was not the direction that he wanted to head in. He explained that he was pulling out of the project and would be obtaining his own separate space sometime in the future.

What was once a three man operation had suddenly become a tag-team. Of course, that also meant that the responsibility of the gallery was also on only the two of us so we both had to pick up what was left on the table and add more to each of our plates. The biggest dilemma wasn't even having to split the rent and other expenses two ways instead of three which was obviously more stressful. The biggest dilemma was that the artist out of the group, the only one who created visual art at the time and knew other artists who could help fill the empty walls of the gallery had left and taken all of his skills, knowledge, experience, and relationships with him. Prior to him leaving my agreed upon personal responsibility was mainly marketing, promotions, and obtaining sponsorships. The artist was to take care of anything art related. I had planned to just walk into the gallery and say "Wow, that's nice".

Now, I know that you do not know me personally, but I assure you that I do not sell wolf tickets. So if I say there's a wolf then there is a wolf. That means if I say I am going to do something barring ill health, debilitating handicaps, or forces of nature outside of my control then I am going to do it. If I do not possess what resources and/or knowledge I need at that moment then I will obtain it one way or another in order to deliver. I am that determined.

I had to learn about art. Filing new paperwork with the state and changing the business name on the lease were more easily handled matters. You cannot be an art gallery without art. You cannot be an art gallery without relationships with any artists. This is especially true if you are not an artist yourself with enough work to fill your space. I had to learn about art.

What did I do? I visited well over fifteen art galleries within the two months of renovation between getting the keys to our space and our grand opening. I was at every opening reception where artists would be present. I was at every artist talk and art council meeting in the state. We even jumped on the road and drove all the way from New Jersey to North Carolina to witness the grand opening of another art gallery owned by an up and coming artist who was quickly rising to stardom and has since opened a newer and even larger art gallery due to her success.

My partner and I read books (none as good as this one) and met and talked with as many artists as we could find. We asked them as many questions as we could come up with mainly about their experiences with galleries. We were most interested in hearing about the bad experiences so that way we could eliminate wasted time, avoidable mistakes, and failed or strained relationships with artists. It was during this time that I befriended a man who I would later learned was the legendary Jerry Gant (Newark, NJ) who painted with and was friends with Jean-Michel Basqiuat. Jerry became a mentor to me and his colorful theories called "Gantalism" were always insightful, hilarious, and coated with pain, love and wisdom. Rest in peace Jerry Gant.

My former partner has since gone wholly back into music and left the visual art sid eto myself. I have sacrificed a lot and dedicated myself to my dream. I have acquired much more experience and knowledge in the last six years than I had realized until I started thinking about putting this book together. I still have a ways to go on my journey based on my ambitions but I have come so far and witnessed so many others fail along the way.

As many mistakes as I have avoided I still made many others and some of these have been my greatest teachers. This is especially true about the mistakes that cost me money. It's kind of hard to forget those. I went from knowing very little about art (other than I appreciated it) to owning a consistently profitable and distinguished art gallery that has artists banging at our doors and flooding our inboxes to be exhibited. I find ourselves giving interviews, receiving awards, having articles written about us and patrons who make sure almost all of our events are sold out.

As a gallerist, arts administrator, and visual artist myself I understand the artworld from a few different perspectives. I understand that each of these positions play a role in moving the cogs in the industry and all need each other to truly thrive. Yes, artists of all mediums can potentially go direct to consumers but most lack the organizational, management, and frankly, professional skills that it takes to put on large scale productions.

With that being said, I have written this book specifically for the individual artist. The one who has to sell most of their works themselves, find all the shows themselves, and create income and opportunity all on their own. This book will help you increase your results. Everything learned here will add to your toolbelt and used at the right time will get the job done.

Acknowledgments

There is a large group of supporters who invested in the production of this book. Without their monetary support and belief that I could deliver a quality product, this book might not exist. I want to give them shoutouts so that they are forever memorialized as a part of my journey and growth. They are artists and more importantly, they are comrades in this art life.

Jazlyne Wooden	Diane Bainton	Shima Bhamra
Amanda Jackson	Ayah Davis-Karim	Dana Powell-Smith
Stephanie Gowdy	Krista Swisher	Christina Velasquez
Qeshia Ward	Cydney Wilson	Isjanee Barnes
Daishanna Pearson	Daniel Leighton	Rachel Rawlins
Charles Hill	Kervin Andre	Ron Powell
Nicole Durham	Lewis Guy	Patrick Henry
Delana Gray	Kicherra Chisolm	Kenya Henry
Cent Jones	Chantrice Copeland	Darian Tucker
Kaila Boulware-Sykes	Raymond Sykes	Jayde Greene
Kween Moore	Taleya Johnson	Sasha-Loriene
Joli McTerrell	Cindy Cephas	Warren Hynson
Davynte Pannell	Melissa Suggs	Bianca J Jackson
Carmen Serra-Luna	Valencia Wilson	Helen Ellis
Ameerah Shabazz-Bilal	Cory Ford	Jona Taylor

Also huge shout to my professional artist fraternity, **Gamma Xi Phi**

Table of Contents

Introduction

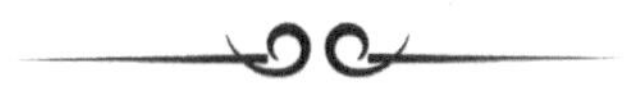

So, I actually haven't done the math nor have I bothered to research data on approximately how many visual artists are more introverted than extroverted. After writing that sentence I just realized that there will be many introverted artists that would avoid taking a survey to discover accurate statistics anyway. I am still going to take a guess based on my encounters and experiences even though I know how limited they are in comparison to the number of artists in this world at this present time, let alone in history.

If I had to guess, which I do for the purposes of this book, I would say that approximately 70% of visual artists are introverts. I would further argue that there are more introverts amongst visual artists than performing artists because visual artists have the option of showcasing their work a lot more than themselves and the performance of their work. The performance, in essence, is the finished product, and the artist can retreat to solitude or within themselves during the process.

I am writing this book to help those introverted artists, primarily, use who they are to get what they want and ultimately need; art sales. There is no need to become something that you are not. This book is about recognizing your superpower as an introvert and putting it into action. I mean what fun would invisibility be if people could see you all the time? It would be a waste of a superpower. If you practice executing the knowledge in this book your superpower can bring you super profit. Every animal with one comes out of its shell to eat. Let's ensure that when you pop out of your shell, albeit momentarily, you do just that, eat!

Artists typically don't have an easy time selling their work consistently and successfully. Not wanting to "bother" people means that artists don't often ask or they do the dreaded "link in my bio" and call it a day. Most artists just want "to art". That is, they just want to create. They don't want to have to always be creating content, figuring out who their ideal client avatars are, coming up with copyrighting to sell their pieces, etc. Having to sell the work is a whole other job for an artist.

The better you get at marketing the less you have to worry about selling but the better you get at selling less of your marketing money gets wasted through squandered opportunities. Customer concerns would be addressed, objections would be overturned, upsales or order bumps would be made, and connections would be made that would increase the likelihood of return sales and/or referrals. So to be best equipped to reach your goals as an independent visual artist is to become very adept at both sales and marketing.

I, as an artist myself, understand that we want our art to speak for itself. Even if it could speak for itself, how many languages can it speak? Does it know the nuances and the slang of the language? Is it persuasive or just pretty? Even if it could do all that literal talking there's something it definitely can't do. It cannot listen.

It takes listening to make the connection to most buyers/collectors. This is one of the superpowers of introverted artists. Unlocking all your gifts and seeing them as strengths instead of weaknesses is the first step to setting your art sales on a new path and trajectory toward financial success.

Learning how to speak and write about your art in a way that allows potential buyers, collectors, and clients to realize its value helps them realize that they need your art in their lives. Learning how to get them to do most of the speaking and still being able to accomplish this task is where this book comes in.

Whether selling direct in-person, online, independently or through representation we all want to move more work and get more art out there. Even if you want to be in museums most of them get their art from private collections. The art is usually purchased by the collector and then added to the private collection so it still starts with a sale.

Most artists sell their work independently through their own platforms. Most of these platforms are digital. Many artists either haven't built up a substantial email list or if they have an email list they don't know how to nurture those potential customers and get them to feel like they know, actually like, and can trust the artist enough to purchase when they're ready to purchase. The skills in this book can also be used here to increase passive sales through your automated email server and email list.

After reading this book you should be able to:

> Increase your closing ratio

> Increase your prices

> Increase your average sales order

> Get people to sell to themselves so you don't have to

Are You Introverted Or Are You Shy?

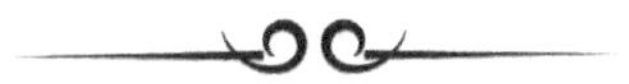

Have you ever thought about that? Have you really examined yourself? What is the answer? Are you both? In case you didn't know there is definitely a difference between the two. I'm not big on judgment but for the sake of scholarship, I will say that it is another task to overcome shyness on top of navigating your introversion.

It's not that one is better than the other but, with introverts, you at least have pockets of socialization and can open up to people you feel comfortable around. Let's get some clarity on how I'm personally defining these terms so that we are on the same page. These words are sometimes misused or misunderstood and we would be better off viewing these concepts as follows:

Introvert - Feels more comfortable focusing on their inner thoughts and ideas, rather than what's happening externally. They become easily overstimulated and need to be alone to regain energy after spending time with people. They enjoy spending time with one or two people rather than with larger crowds.

Shy - Being reserved or showing or having timidity or nervousness in the presence of other people. There is typically a tendency towards avoidance.

Shyness involves fear of negative evaluation whereas introversion refers to a tendency toward becoming overstimulated and the need to be alone to regain energy. So now that we are clear on how I am differentiating these terms let's get the shyness out of the way now, for those that are both, because the rest of this book will focus on navigating introversion in your sales.

7 Simple Steps To Overcome Shyness

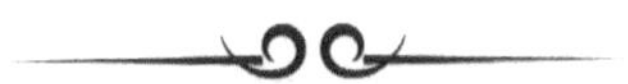

Make A Fear Scale

Make it from 1-10 and list your fears and place them where they fall on the scale. Start overcoming the lower numbers first and gradually move up as you gain more confidence.

Get Familiar With Unfamiliarity

Make a point to visit new environments. The more experienced you become with unfamiliarity, the easier it will be to handle it.

Coin Your Phrase

Rehearsing makes you feel more comfortable. Work on your introduction questions and your brand clarity statement.

Direct Your Attention Outward

Shy people tend to be self-absorbed (no judgment). This does not mean that they are necessarily narcissistic but since they spend so much time with themselves that is where the majority of their focus is. Be observant and compassionate to others around you while in public. It will increase the connection and subsequently the comfort level. You will be so distracted by other people you might even forget that you used to be shy.

Rearrange Your Expectations

Being "super social" might be unrealistic for your personality type. That does not mean that there isn't a bunch of levels in between " super social" and where you are now.

Conquer One New Challenge

One step at a time. It won't all click overnight. Challenge yourself with something new every day. Try to say "hi" to 20 strangers today. Nothing else, just smile and say "hi". No expectations for them to respond at all. This is about you.

Eliminate Scape Goats

Don't use "work" or "lack of a hot outfit" to avoid challenging yourself and growing. Even if it's for an hour, step away and stretch yourself.

Are You Selling To The Right People?

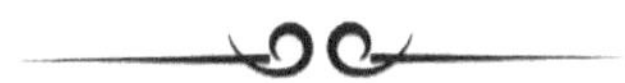

No matter how good you get at selling with these new skills you will get from this book it will not matter if you are attempting to sell to the wrong people. Someone won't typically purchase something they deem as having no value. If they don't want it you probably couldn't even give it away to them, let alone get them to buy it. So before we waste our valuable time and knowledge we need to make sure we are talking to the right people.

Do you know who your best customers are likely to be? When I say best I mean your ideal customer. A customer that haggles and undervalues your work is not an ideal customer. An ideal customer is not only one that wants your offerings but also one that can afford to pay for them and is happy that they get to do it.

Your client avatar is a representation of your ideal client and your target audience for your marketing. Creating a client avatar helps you to understand your ideal client on a deeper level. It clearly defines your niche and helps you to hone your messaging, sales pitch, content, and pretty much every other element of your financial planning practice. I guarantee you have a niche of some sort – you probably just haven't framed it that way yet. That's what this client avatar process can help you do!

By uncovering the deeper fears, goals, and values of your ideal client, you're creating a psychographic niche. Your clients may span a wide range of ages, professions, locations, and more – but more than likely, there's a consistent thread that ties them together and makes them your ideal clients.

It will be a particular age group, gender, class, race, education level, etc. They will have particular interests and are in a particular situation. These factors will help you locate them. If you can't find them you can't talk to them. The more you know about your ideal client avatar, the easier it will be to connect with them and market to them. If you can figure out why they like your work you can double down on that and find more customers just like that one.

Knowing who you are talking to means knowing how to talk to them and where they are. If you know where they are you can send your marketing messages directly to where they are instead of spending money to send your messages to places where it's not well received. The best marketing and copywriting won't help if they're going to the wrong place and to the wrong people.

It is important to figure out this person's details and be as specific as possible. Do not give them a large age range.

Twenty-year-olds do not hang out at the same places as forty-year-olds unless we are talking about places of worship. So you wouldn't target these two the same. They probably don't use the same vernacular either, being from different eras. We want to make this person as real as possible. No real person has a twenty-year age range. They are one age! Give them an age.

Since selling isn't high on most introverts' list of fun things to do in their spare time, you want to do as little of it as possible. So instead of worrying about having to sell to many people in order to be successful just focus on only selling to one person. This person, your ideal client avatar, is the representation of others like them that also want your offerings. If you can reach that one person then you can reach others just like them.

Focusing on what that one person might need and tailoring all your messages directly to them will also help you come up with the messages. Trying to please one person is a lot easier than trying to please many people. Write to them to help them with a particular challenge or pain.

You can plug your client avatar into several places, both internally and in a client-facing way. When you create the client avatar to be a story, people are more likely to connect with you and to view your services as tailor-fit to their needs.

Finding out who your ideal client avatar is typically discovered through one of two ways; You can look at your what it is you do, who you do it for, and what makes you different and focus on the people you do it for or; the alternative route would be to just go out and make sales, see who purchased, note the commonalities between them, and then seek out more people who have those things in common.

If the pool of people that you are trying to sell to is not large enough then you are not selling to the right people. If you have a product that only 1,000 people want then you will probably not make more than 1,000 sales. Even if your art is $1,000 you will be capped at $1,000,000. Now, I know one million sounds like a decent amount of money to make off of your art but the reality is that the 1,000 sales will not all come at once. It is much more likely that these are the numbers that will be produced over the entire duration of your creating your art. $1,000,000.00 in a year is great but $1,000,000.00 over 25-30 years is only $33,333,33 annually. That's a regular entry-level non-degree holding job. That's cool, too, if that is what you want but for me personally, the stress I might encounter and the energy and effort it would take to make that same amount of money might not be worth it.

Are the people that you are attempting to sell able to purchase what you're selling? Even if they wanted to buy it but didn't have the income or means to do it they cannot effectively buy whatever you're selling. This would mean that you're selling to the wrong people. You might be trying to sell a Mercedes to people with Honda budgets. You will be much more successful if you went and found and/or attracted Mercedes buyers.

Attracting Your Ideal Client Avatar

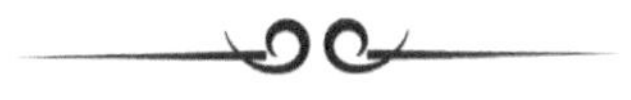

Now that we have identified our Ideal Client Avatar we have to bring them to us. How do we do that? We talk nice to them. Not only do we talk nice to them but we say it in their language. What do I mean by that? I mean more specifically their vernacular, their lingo. This is the way that they will identify you as one of them. If you are one of them then you might understand their pains or needs.

For example, one artist I work with, Justice, identifies as queer. His artwork explores that lifestyle and what comes with it, i.e., freedom, fluidity, rejection from friends/family, hate speech, feeling alienated or misunderstood, etc. After I was educated we decided it was best to use the lingo of the community so if they happened to scroll past or see a few words or an image they would know to stop scrolling and pay attention because the message is speaking directly to them. Words like; drab, gaff and crash-landing were used to great effect to cut through the noise of countless ads and posts fighting for your attention.

Your avatar has a problem and something that you have is the solution to that problem. You just have to make sure they know you have it. You can offer a sample of this solution or the whole solution in the form of a **lead magnet** to attract the lead to you. A lead magnet is a marketing term for a free/low-cost item or service that is given away for the purpose of gathering contact information for future marketing.

Lead magnets can work for you even when you are not working them as long as traffic is being driven to them. Lead magnets form a bridge of awareness or exposure to likability and trust. If you did not know the three factors that lead people to buy they are; know, like, and trust. A great lead magnet can take care of the last two definitely and possibly all three. Feeling like you know someone or some brand comes with consistency and may take a little longer to make people feel like they know your brand.

Once you have created a call to action to consume the lead magnet, i.e., "Click the link above" or "Visit the website now" the customer starts on that journey. The first place they should visit will be your landing page. Here they will give you the required information, i.e., name, email, and phone number. Once they input their information they will receive the lead magnet. I would recommend that you automate this process. (You can use Mailerlite to set up a landing page and email automation for a deep discount using this link www.mailerlite.com/a/rix6cj2glj)

Your lead magnets will not work if they are not targeted. Not only that, but the information you do get might not be of much use to you. For example, let us say your lead magnet was a calendar and you were giving away a free digital download of the calendar. If this is a calendar with general images but you paint in specific themes you might find people who love the free calendar but are not interested in your work so marketing to them is useless. In reality, getting them on your marketing list might greatly decrease your return on investment.

On the other hand, if you painted historic figures or focused on themes of Black love and you created a Black Love calendar or a history calendar then most of the people who will sign up to receive your lead magnet would also be interested in purchasing some of your artwork.

Popular lead magnet examples; Lists, Checklists, Surveys, Ebooks, Webinars, Newsletters, Templates, Calendars, Trials, etc.

What Makes A Good Lead Magnet?

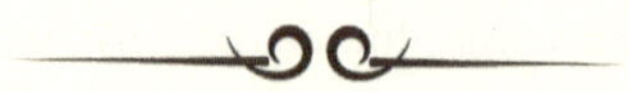

All great lead magnets cover one, if not more of these functions. They either educate, entertain, or remedy a problem. The best do all three. There are common factors that all the most effective lead magnets share regardless of what the industry or who the ideal client avatar is.

Specificity: For a Lead Magnet to perform well, it needs to solve a specific problem by offering a specific solution for a specific segment of your market.

Instant Gratification: A high-converting Lead Magnet must also be instantly valuable to the consumer. Audiences want a solution to their problems immediately, so the quicker you can give it to them—the better.

Unique Value: Of course, your business won't be the only one using Lead Magnets to get customer information, so it's important that you offer something unique. A customer should be convinced that you are the right business to buy from over your competitors.

Here you should focus on the value proposition. This is the value you promise to deliver to customers should they choose to buy from you at some point. It's like the sample food on the toothpick at the mall. You know you are going to get more of that same taste if you actually buy.

High Perceived Value/High Actual Value: Just because something is free doesn't mean it should look free. Your lead magnet needs to be high-quality information that your customer is dying to know. Being that we are creatives it should not be too hard to make it aesthetically pleasing. (If you can't make it pretty ask a friend)

Location on their customer journey: The same lead magnet that might attract a new customer might not be the one that gets them to buy. If they have never heard of you before there is very little risk to giving an email in exchange for information. Most people have to get more familiar with you before they part with their money though.

A freebie can get them into your funnel but it might take a discount code sent out to all those who got the freebie to get them to become actual customers. If you send out a discount code first and you have not established your value it might not mean much. 90% off of something someone doesn't want isn't really a deal.

Make Yourself Easy To Find

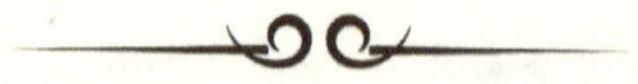

Now that we know what we do, how we do it, what makes us different, and who we are selling to we can focus on making it easier for people to find us. Marketing is all about visibility. You can have the best products in the world but if no one knows how great they are, or that they even exist, no one will buy them. How can they? They don't know they exist. If they have heard about you/them but they cannot find you then you have the same problem.

Being found is being discovered. The beauty is in today's age there are a bunch of tools that help with discovery. Outside of search engines themselves i.e. Google, Bing, Duck Duck Go, etc., a lot of platforms have search engines included in them. When you search for a title, topic, or hashtag on Instagram, Facebook, Tiktok, Twitter, etc. anyone or anything associated with that search can potentially be discovered.

You would be surprised how many artists do not have the word "artist" in their profiles anywhere at all. So anyone who is looking for an artist will have great difficulty coming across this person if they only used that search word. This is the exact opposite of making yourself easy to find. (Side note; make sure all of your artist accounts are public!).

Art is sold every single day. There were approximately $65.1 billion dollars in art sales in 2021. This number only reports the dealers and auction houses. There were a ton of artists also making private and/or direct sales to customers and the lockdown during the pandemic helped people come back to art so there is no better time than now that has been before for the individual artist. There are people who already want to buy what you have to sell. You just have to close the gap between them and yourself.

Awareness is the first step in any sales funnel. If people do not know you or your products exist it's difficult to sell those products to them. Even if you spend money running advertisements to build awareness you still run across the next problem of not having a reputation. A reputation takes time to build. During that time being both consistent and prolific is the key.

If someone was courting you it would probably be easy to gauge their interest level by how often they contacted you, the things they said to you, and the time they spend with you. You are courting your prospects or potential customers. Keeping this in mind you cannot show up once a month or every other week. This makes you unpredictable and thus less reliable. If you're not reliable how reliable will people believe your products or services are?

You have to create a lot of content and it has to consistently be aligned with your core values and your client's needs/wants/desires. Having a lot of underwhelming content only tells them that you're not good at what you do. Putting advertisements on this content will only tell even more people that you're not good at what you do. Because of this what you put out is just as important as the frequency of your output.

Create content that teaches people something that they didn't know. This could be about you, your product, their pain points, etc. Teaching is one of the fastest ways to build authority. If you are considered an authority in what you do you are deemed more trustworthy. If I can trust you then I can trust that what you are telling me about your products or services is true. Once they buy into you they usually buy what you are selling too.

If you are having difficulty creating profound content you can find some profound content that is underdeveloped and develop it in a way that your ideal client avatar will easily understand. Expand old ideas or update them to the current times. Nothing is really new under the sun anyway. What is new is how you look at things. Perspective is reality.

The next thing is to be prolific. You have to produce content. Whichever platform(s) you decide to use has to be filled with content. Don't forget that this is the profound content we're talking about. This is important because once someone does discover you they will then research you. They will go over anything they see on the platforms that they discovered you on and binge on your content if it is profound. Then they can better ascertain whether or not they want to buy into you by buying your product or service.

This is basic human behavior. Think about it. When you discover a show that you like on Netflix, Hulu, or wherever, you binge on the show. You go back and watch all the episodes from all the seasons because you're into the story. Each episode delivers more of the same content that you like in the first episode you saw or heard about from a reputable source. Your content should be episodic.

Skills To Get Better At Sales

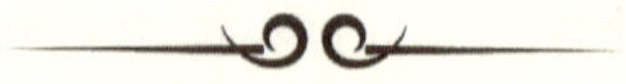

- ➢ **Learn Psychology** - Remember that most people do not want to be sold, they want to buy. All you have to do is create the conditions for them to do so. Figure out what would make their decision easier. How can you get them to think out loud in front of you? Manage their perceptions of loss and fairness.

- ➢ **Practice Empathy** - Empathy requires paying close attention to the specific words others use and their body language. This can allow you to read what they are not saying but feel or believe. Noticing the feelings that arise with us when we interact with people and asking them about their feelings regularly helps us refine our capacity to accurately sense others' emotional experiences.

- ➢ **Increase Charisma** - Luckily, since charisma is a collection of behaviors, you can actually learn it. You can work on developing self-confidence, empathy, and assertiveness. Pay close attention to what your own body language is saying, and smile as much as genuinely possible when you are around people. Make people feel important in the conversation. Remember not to talk at them, but only to talk to them.

- Pace your speech
- Practice eye contact
- Ask clarifying questions
- Remember little details

➤ **Become Confident** - Confidence is an emotional state of mind. It is the perspective that you lack nothing. Practice self-assured body language; stand up straight, square your shoulders, and lift your chin. Make a list of positive qualities.

➤ **Study Persuasion** - To start improving your persuasion skills, first assess whether or not you yourself have an open mind. If you are not open it is more difficult to understand what it means to be open-minded, how open-minded people respond/behave, and how to persuade them. Ask people whom you regularly interact with if you are open-minded. If they say, "no", then start the work there.

Some methods and techniques for more success in persuasion; establishing your credibility, being well prepared, understanding your avatar's interests, emotional connection, unexpected honesty, remembering exactly what they said and repeating it, and mirroring.

➤ **Product Expertise** - What's special or unique about your product or service? If it is paintings, what materials are you using? What is the quality of those materials as compared to materials typically used by most artists? Will this last longer? Is it more durable? Is it flame-retardant? Is it waterproof? Is the paint non-toxic and family-friendly? Is it museum quality? All of this knowledge of your product helps sell your product.

Proving knowledge of your product also helps build trust that you are recommending the right product for the right person instead of just trying to sell anything to anyone that will buy. People want to know/feel like what they are purchasing will serve them specifically. We all know what works for one might not necessarily work for another. If you know what you have and you demonstrate that you know what they need they are more likely to accept your solution.

➢ **Relationship Building** - The ability to build relationships is critical for anyone selling anything. Relationships lead to referrals and repeat business. The higher the price point or perceived value of the product the more the potential buyers want to establish trust with those they are buying from.

➢ **Following Up** - Approximately 94% of people do not buy the first time they visit a new website or store. While we want to make sure we get the 6% that is ready to purchase right now, we definitely cannot just let the much larger number go. These people might not be ready to buy at this moment but at some point, they will be ready and you want to be top of mind when they are. How do you do that? You follow up. You stay in contact. You continue to build the "know, like, and trust factors" involved in making sales.

7 Steps To Master The Art Of Persuasion

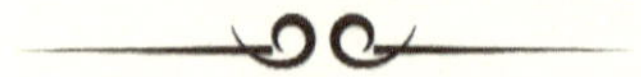

Repetition, Repetition, Repetition.

Should I repeat it again? Repetition is the key to getting people's attention. Many people have developed filters to ignore unsolicited input until they discern whether or not it's for them. If you repeat it to them it becomes more apparent that you are.

Postulate the message in a context important to the receiver.

Avoid abstract or technical declarations that may sound like an effort to impress or mislead your audience with your intelligence. Use specific value propositions rather than fuzzy terms like "easier", "better" or "faster".

Use contrasting story scenarios to illustrate the impact.

Tell stories wherever you can instead of simple statements of fact. Try to integrate the listener or receiver directly into the story. The power of contrast or side-by-side comparison of outcomes is an effective mover of people from old beliefs to new ones.

Personalize your message.

Serve the same dish just add different garnishes to it. Be sure to listen first to find a personal intersection of interest with your idea/product and the person. If a person is intuitive and creative, do not use a logical and analytical message to try to reach them. The more information you can gather through listening or prior research, the better equipped you will be.

Warm introductions or personal referrals

Everyone is more prone to listen and believe new people brought to them by someone they know in common, especially if that connection is respected and has strong relevant experience or expertise in that specific area. It might take longer to arrange a meeting, in some cases, but your closing rate will thank you.

Present evidence of interest and excitement from others

Even if it is just people signing up for your waiting list it let people know that it's happening. It can show excitement and people want to be where the excitement is. Action creates action. Shout out to the people who are participating. Post pictures of people receiving goods or lining up at your booth or store. Proof of real customers who have paid full price for your art/art services with high customer satisfaction shows business execution tracking.

Recapitulate

Repeat back to them the exact words they used when talking to you to show them that you have been listening intently and that what they said was important enough to remember. Listening implies that you care which builds trust in believing that you can meet their needs/solve their problem.

5 Words You Should Never Say In sales

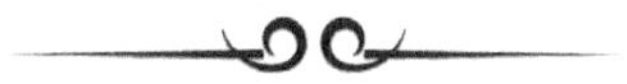

"Cost"

The word cost can cost you. Just like when your energy is spent when your money is spent, it's gone. You had to give it up so you lost something. People are happier when they "invest". This term brings anticipation of the investment becoming fruitful and being worth even more than what the initial investment was. Investment is a higher vibrational word and leaves hope with the prospect. They understand that the transaction will benefit them more than it will benefit you, even though you're selling it to them.

"Objection"

Get into the habit of viewing what might seem like objections merely as concerns. Objections can lead to resistance and arguments. You will find yourself trying to convince someone to buy. Concerns can be peacefully addressed and the prospect can be reassured. If you receive any objections ask them, "what is your concern, exactly?"

"Cheap"

This word subconsciously speaks to quality more than it does to price. People imagine it breaking or looking worn quickly and not lasting long enough for them to get the value out of their purchase. People do not want cheap products or services. People want a deal. They want something worth a lot but they might not necessarily want to pay a lot. So we don't say cheap even when we're giving a deal. Instead, we use terms like "cost-effective" or "budget-friendly".

"Contract"

The prefix "con" implies trickery and the possibility of being tied up legally for long periods or possibly perpetuity. Use the word "agreement" instead. There is more ease and connotations to go along and less finality to it.

"Buy"

Paint the picture (pun intended) that they already have purchased and they are experiencing the benefits already. Use the word "own" instead.

Two Ears And One Mouth

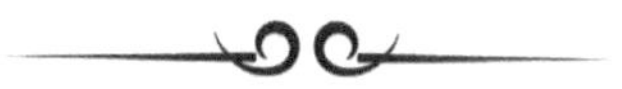

I'm sure you've heard this saying before. It is about how we should use the gifts given to us in proportion. We have more ears so that would be an indication that hearing was so important the creator doubled down on ears. Since we only have one mouth it should be used less than ears are used. That's what introverts do naturally.

Being an introvert is a huge advantage in sales. Introverts tend to be quiet. Being quiet allows them the space to listen to their prospect instead of just waiting for their prospect to finish talking so that they can get a word in, like a lot of salespeople. Extroverts naturally want to talk and might not gather enough information to make a natural connection to the prospect.

Introverts tend to be intuitive and observational. They can get people talking to take up the conversation all the while picking up on things not even being said directly that can give them more insight into any connections or concerns of the prospect. Once the concerns are identified they can be focused on and addressed. This helps make a lasting and profitable connection with prospects.

To effectively manipulate emotions you need to be able to read emotions. I don't know about you but I have never been able to both read something and talk about something else simultaneously. I have personally had a high reading level since elementary school and have taken honors and advanced placement classes and I still never learned how to do that. It's not possible, at least not if you actually want to comprehend and also remember what it is you were reading while you are talking about something other than what you are reading.

It is almost impossible to persuade someone to change their mind or take a direct or implied suggestion to take action if you have not made them feel understood. It is difficult to understand someone that you never listened to.

If you are paying attention you can see when someone's weight shifts or their body language or tone of voice changes throughout the conversation indicating to you how they are feeling at that moment and how close they are to saying "yes" to the sale. When you notice something, address it. This can exhibit that you are tuned in to the prospect and are there to **serve rather than sell**.

Repeat parts of what they have said for ensuring clarity and demonstrating that you were actually listening to them and understanding them. Make sure you are facing the speaker and making eye contact. Do not interrupt them speaking, even if you're excited. Hold that thought! Don't plan what to say next. You won't know what to say next if you weren't paying attention to what was said before. If you never get to say what you had planned to say but you still make the sale, does it matter? I didn't think so. Say what needs to be said and only what needs to be said. Don't say everything.

Listen Listen Listen

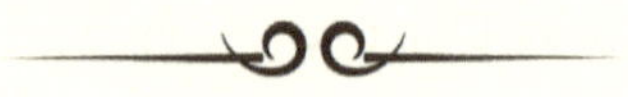

Many of the tactics I have previously mentioned will not actually work without this piece here. One of the beautiful things about introverted people is that they have no problem letting other people talk. When this is happening we have to be sure to be listening and not just waiting for them to be silent long enough for us to say our next lines. What if they ask a question or make a comment that has nothing to do with what you have planned to say next?

You have to address what they asked or commented about before you can get back to your script/speech/spiel. Otherwise, they won't feel heard and it will become more of a sales transaction than you simply providing a solution. Imagine if someone was talking about the different hues of blue you used in a painting and you responded by talking about how you stretched the canvas yourself. While that is an interesting fact and can possibly swing someone over the fence by demonstrating the hand-crafted high-quality the timing is off it can easily also turn the potential customer off.

Active listening skills are your best friend. Even if you are not sure what to say next, just listening to what they are saying now will take you there. Where is there? Wherever it is that they needed to go in order to buy in. Your ability to both listen to and understand your prospects can make or break your ability to win the sale. Not only does active listening help you clarify what it is that your potential customer is looking for or what sways them, but it also establishes absolutely necessary trust with your prospects.

When the customers feel heard and listened to (not the same thing), it creates a connection that can keep the sales process moving in the direction of the sale. Don't just ramble off reasons why they should buy. Listen to what they want and then list the reasons why what you have is what they want.

Don't Sell. Help people buy.

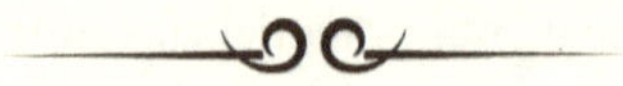

Don't worry about your sales pitch so much. Actually, other than knowing about your product thoroughly, you might benefit from not actually having a sales pitch at all. When you do have a sales pitch you can sometimes feel thrown off when someone interrupts your pitch. Sometimes starting it again at the spot you left off before the interruption does not flow with the conversation. When that happens it becomes even more apparent (not that you were hiding it) that you are just trying to sell what you have to anyone that will buy whether they actually need it to serve a purpose or not. People don't want to be sold. People want to buy!

If people had absolutely no interest in what it is that you are selling they would dismiss or ignore you as soon as you spoke or the moment that they came across your content. The fact that they are still in your presence or still corresponding to your follow-up is a sign of interest. Now your job is to find out exactly what about it interests them and focus on that part. No other parts matter, even though they exist.

If I am selling a car and my prospect is talking about how vehicles can go and how they handle the road at high speeds all of my conversations are going to be around that. That is what excites the prospect. If they're not excited then they're bored. When you are bored you change the channel or tune out of the conversation. W do not want that to happen! Don't be boring. Be exciting!

Questions To Dig Deeper

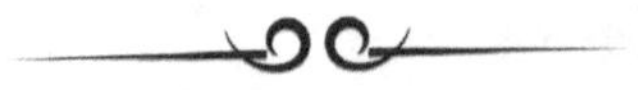

The more questions that you ask the more information you can gather. The more information you gather the more ammunition that you have to use to quire your target and close the sale. Asking questions can help the prospect better understand themselves and their wants and needs also, so it's a win-win situation for everyone. They get something they really like and you get the sale. Below are some questions to ask to keep the conversation going and to gather more information from your prospect that can help you all out during the transaction. These can be used at almost any part of the conversation and can definitely come in handy if the conversation is stalling. They are not in any particular order.

What do you mean?

Can you give me some examples?

Why are these your favorites?

What do you like about it?

Who are your favorite artists?

What if you could get one of your favorite artist's pieces before they became famous?

How would you feel if you discovered the next (insert their favorite artist's name) before anyone else?

What thoughts do you have when you look at this piece?

What feelings does it make you feel?

Where in your personal space can you use that energy?

How much do you think it's worth and how much should you pay for it?

Mistakes To Avoid

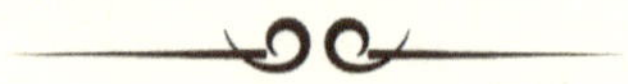

- ➤ Talking about the price too soon - Speak on benefits first. Paint the picture of ownership before you ask them to own it. If asked about the price early, respond, " Oh, you like it? What do you like about it". This will allow you to gather more information while simultaneously getting the prospect to remind themselves of why your product is so amazing.

- ➤ Talking about features instead of benefits - People often forget that there are many benefits to owning and viewing art. While people care about what it looks like they care even more about what it makes them think and how it makes them feel.

- ➤ Trying too hard to sell - You have to find the right balance between getting your point across and not pushing your prospect into a corner. Get better at positioning yourself and the offer value.

- ➤ Don't agree with them all of the time - This creates distrust because it lacks authenticity. People respect honesty and trust honest people. It is ok to have a difference of opinion.

➢ Not putting emotion in your offer - Let your prospect picture walking into the house and leaving their stress at the door, right next to your painting.

➢ Stop trying to get married on the first date - Get to know them first. They will eventually tell you what they like, so you can focus on that, and what they don't like, so you won't make those same mistakes. Don't try to sell with the first message or the first words out of your mouth.

The Impulse Factors

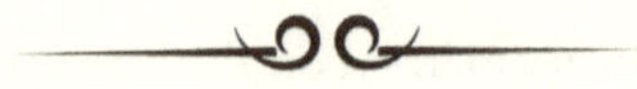

So I am sure that you have noticed that simply offering a big discount on your art rarely drives the sales you expected. What then? Do you just keep running sales more frequently and/or with deeper discounts further lowering the perceived value of your work?

People buy when they're ready to buy or when they're impulsed to buy. If you can stimulate these impulses you will find yourself making many more sales and much more money. The good thing about making more sales is that it builds confidence by affirming that people want what it is you have and that confidence then brings in even more sales.

One of the most powerful tools to trigger impulse to purchase immediately is impulse marketing. These are psychological factors to influence customers, trigger the right reaction and deliver the sales you expect. Mastering each of these will seriously elevate your game.

Fear of Loss - "If they don't get it now either the product or the deal will be gone forever!"

Nobody wants to miss out on a good deal. I even found myself a victim of this. I recently purchased a trumpet at a garage sale that I happened to drive-by just because it was almost brand new and it was only $40. I haven't played a trumpet in 12 years but it was "only $40". I had to grab it! I haven't played a note yet. I plan to but we'll see what happens. I'll update you in the next book.

This is a part of what is known as "FOMO" or "fear of missing out". This is driven by the psychological need not to lose out. Because being left out is considered used to mean we missed a meal or something that is still programmed in us for safety and survival. We actually have a part of our brain that is specialized for sensing when we are being leftout.

Not having vital information or getting the impression that one is not a part of the group or an outsider can have damaging effects physically and psychologically. Not being in the "in" group is enough for many people's limbic systems to engage in the "fight or flight" response.

Psychological stress does not feel good and the fear of missing out brings that stress out of most people and most people want to avoid it. In an attempt to prevent experiencing the stress, some people will redouble their efforts to not miss out on anything and therefore get everything.

When marketing or sending offers to your customers it is important to periodically remind or inform them of the reasons why they need to buy from you now or possibly miss out forever!

- ➤ Make your offer time specific

- ➤ Have a limited quantity

- ➤ Create exclusivity

Sense of Urgency - Taking action promptly.

It is common to hear someone say, "I'll think about it". The chances of them coming back are usually slim. Now, if they are thinking about how to purchase the item, i.e., moving funds around, then that is different. How do you get them to make unplanned purchases possible? Create a sense of urgency. Essentially, everything else they had planned or had funds previously advocated for can wait because this purchase needs to happen right there snd then.

Scarcity is a piece of this and psychologists have proven that creating a sense of scarcity also triggers people to buy. Remember when we got locked down during quarantine and all of the toilet paper was gone? Exactly! You probably grabbed a few extra rolls for yourself just in case the madness left no toilet paper.

With art, buyers often feel like they have no immediate need to move forward, despite finding value in it or appreciating it. So, how do you get them to move faster through your sales pipeline? Well, you could create the competitive atmosphere of an art auction or you could try a different route.

Discovering immediate pain is the best way to create a sense of urgency. People want pain to end as soon as possible. Sometimes people don't realize how bad their pain is but it is your job to point it out. Positioning your product as the end of their pain is the shortest path to a sale. The more of the pain people are in, the more they will pay to relieve that path.

Greed Factor - Everyone wants more for less.

This is where you have to convince people that the price that they're paying for the product is lower than the actual value of the product. It's the equivalent of buying a home with positive equity already built into the purchase price.

One way to do this can be to state the original price and then state the discount with a justificition of the discount and then stating the amount saved.

The Jones' Effect/Social Proof -

For most of the public the next best thing to being popular is to have what popular people have or to do what is popular and trending. It is popular because other people have it. Often, people want what other people have. This method can make people feel out of touch with what is trending and motivate them to make a purchase in order to "keep up with the Joneses".

People often feel inferior if they can't keep up. Including social proof like pictures of purchases and testimonials show that you are trendy and can often motivate someone to purchase from you in order to keep up.

www.ingramcontent.com/pod-product-compliance
Lightning Source LLC
Chambersburg PA
CBHW061405160726
47995CB00001B/477